*GREATER THAN A T(
   ALSO AVAILABLE
       AUDIOBOOK FORMAT.

Greater Than a Tourist Book Series Reviews from Readers

I think the series is wonderful and beneficial for tourists to get information before visiting the city.

-Seckin Zumbul, Izmir Turkey

I am a world traveler who has read many trip guides but this one really made a difference for me. I would call it a heartfelt creation of a local guide expert instead of just a guide.

-Susy, Isla Holbox, Mexico

New to the area like me, this is a must have!

-Joe, Bloomington, USA

This is a good series that gets down to it when looking for things to do at your destination without having to read a novel for just a few ideas.

-Rachel, Monterey, USA

Good information to have to plan my trip to this destination.

-Pennie Farrell, Mexico

Great ideas for a port day.

-Mary Martin USA

Aptly titled, you won't just be a tourist after reading this book. You'll be greater than a tourist!

-Alan Warner, Grand Rapids, USA

Even though I only have three days to spend in San Miguel in an upcoming visit, I will use the author's suggestions to guide some of my time there. An easy read - with chapters named to guide me in directions I want to go.

-Robert Catapano, USA

Great insights from a local perspective! Useful information and a very good value!

-Sarah, USA

This series provides an in-depth experience through the eyes of a local. Reading these series will help you to travel the city in with confidence and it'll make your journey a unique one.

-Andrew Teoh, Ipoh, Malaysia

>TOURIST

GREATER THAN A TOURIST- CAPE TOWN WESTERN CAPE SOUTH AFRICA

50 Travel Tips from a Local

Hendrik Human

Greater Than a Tourist-Cape Town, Western Cape, South Africa Copyright © 2021 by CZYK Publishing LLC. All Rights Reserved.

All rights reserved. No part of this book may be reproduced in any form or by any electronic or mechanical means including information storage and retrieval systems, without permission in writing from the author. The only exception is by a reviewer, who may quote short excerpts in a review.

The statements in this book are of the authors and may not be the views of CZYK Publishing or Greater Than a Tourist.
First Edition
Cover designed by: Ivana Stamenkovic
Cover Image: https://pixabay.com/photos/helicopter-ride-flight-exciting-1218974/

Image 1: By SkyPixels - Own work, CC BY-SA 4.0, https://commons.wikimedia.org/w/index.php?curid=40397200
Image 2: By Warren Rohner - originally posted to Flickr as Clifton 4th Beach, CC BY-SA 2.0, https://commons.wikimedia.org/w/index.php?curid=4316608
Image 3: By Damien du Toit - originally posted to Flickr as Waterfront panorama, CC BY 2.0, https://commons.wikimedia.org/w/index.php?curid=4314413
Image 4: By Andrew Massyn - Own work, Public Domain, https://commons.wikimedia.org/w/index.php?curid=1574559

CZYK
PUBLISHING

CZYK Publishing Since 2011.
CZYKPublishing.com
Greater Than a Tourist

Lock Haven, PA
All rights reserved.
ISBN: 9798730162945

>TOURIST

50 TRAVEL TIPS FROM A LOCAL

BOOK DESCRIPTION

With travel tips and culture in our guidebooks written by a local, it is never too late to visit Cape Town. Greater Than a Tourist-Cape Town, Western Cape, South Africa by author Hendrik Human offers the inside scoop on Cape Town, the Mother City. Most travel books tell you how to travel like a tourist. Although there is nothing wrong with that, as part of the 'Greater Than a Tourist' series, this book will give you candid travel tips from someone who has lived at your next travel destination. This guide book will not tell you exact addresses or store hours but instead gives you knowledge that you may not find in other smaller print travel books. Experience cultural, culinary delights, and attractions with the guidance of a Local. Slow down and get to know the people with this invaluable guide. By the time you finish this book, you will be eager and prepared to discover new activities at your next travel destination.

Inside this travel guide book you will find:

Visitor information from a Local
Tour ideas and inspiration
Save time with valuable guidebook information

Greater Than a Tourist- A Travel Guidebook with 50 Travel Tips from a Local. Slow down, stay in one place, and get to know the people and culture. By the time you finish this book, you will be eager and prepared to travel to your next destination.

>TOURIST

OUR STORY

Traveling is a passion of the Greater than a Tourist book series creator. Lisa studied abroad in college, and for their honeymoon Lisa and her husband toured Europe. During her travels to Malta, an older man tried to give her some advice based on his own experience living on the island since he was a young boy. She was not sure if she should talk to the stranger but was interested in his advice. When traveling to some places she was wary to talk to locals because she was afraid that they weren't being genuine. Through her travels, Lisa learned how much locals had to share with tourists. Lisa created the Greater Than a Tourist book series to help connect people with locals. A topic that locals are very passionate about sharing.

TABLE OF CONTENTS

Book Description
Our Story
Table of Contents
Dedication
About the Author
How to Use This Book
From the Publisher
WELCOME TO > TOURIST
1. Spend Time
2. Be a Responsible Traveller
3. Be Safe
4. Use Local Currency
5. Get Around Cape Town Easily
6. Choose Great Accommodation
7. Bring Something Warm
8. Take an Orientation Tour
9. Check the Wind Before Choosing Your Beach
10. Hike Table Mountain
11. See Sunrise or Sunset on Lion's Head
12. Visit the Penguins
13. Volunteer
14. Go to the Furthest Southwestern Point on the African Continent
15. Visit Robben Island

16. Visit a Local Brewery
17. Visit a Coffee Roaster
18. Take a Foodie Tour
19. Visit a Winery (Or Ten)
20. Braai
21. Walk Bree Street & Enjoy First Thursdays
22. Seek Out the Fresh Seafood
23. Plan a Fine Dining Evening in Cape Town
24. Visit a Local Farmers Market
25. Devour a Steak
26. Grab a Burger
27. Jump Out of a Plane
28. Meet the "Marine Big 5" or Dive with Sharks
29. Paraglide off Lions Head or Signal Hill
30. Soar Through the Mountains at Cape Canopy Tour
31. Catch a Big One
32. Swim with the Seals
33. Learn to Surf
34. Listen to a Sunset Concert in Kirstenbosch Botanical Gardens
35. Watch a Rugby Match at Cape Town Stadium
36. Go for a Run, Walk or Cycle on the Promenade
37. Abseil Table Mountain
38. Go for High Tea
39. Take a Cooking Class in the Bo Kaap

40. See Contemporary African Art
41. Learn About South Africa's Diverse Cultures and History
42. Hear the Noon Gun on Signal Hill
43. Visit Kalk Bay
44. Watch the Sunset From The Ocean
45. Shop Local
46. Enjoy Sundowners on a Rooftop
47. SUP around the V&A Waterfront
48. Fly through The Sky
49. Visit Woodstock
50. Take the Perfect Instagram Photo at Blouberg Beach
51. Bonus Tip – Relax!

TOP REASONS TO BOOK THIS TRIP

Packing and Planning Tips

Travel Questions

Travel Bucket List

NOTES

DEDICATION

This book is dedicated to my dear wife Chrissy who came to South Africa as a tourist, fell in love with South Africa, fell in love with Cape Town and then fell in love with me. Six months after visiting South Africa, Chrissy packed up her house, sold her car, left her job in the USA and moved to Cape Town to be with me. She is the editor of this book and my collaborator for all of life.

ABOUT THE AUTHOR

Hendrik Human is South African born and bred and currently lives in Cape Town. Together with his wife Chrissy and son William, Hendrik runs two tourism businesses, the award-winning Earthstompers Adventures and foodie tour company Cape Food & Wine Tours. Hendrik has been in the tourism industry for the last 20 years and is passionate about South Africa, adventure, outdoors, food, wine and sustainable living and travel.

HOW TO USE THIS BOOK

The *Greater Than a Tourist* book series was written by someone who has lived in an area for over three months. The goal of this book is to help travelers either dream or experience different locations by providing opinions from a local. The author has made suggestions based on their own experiences. Please check before traveling to the area in case the suggested places are unavailable.

Travel Advisories: As a first step in planning any trip abroad, check the Travel Advisories for your intended destination.
https://travel.state.gov/content/travel/en/traveladvisories/traveladvisories.html

\>TOURIST

FROM THE PUBLISHER

Traveling can be one of the most important parts of a person's life. The anticipation and memories that you have are some of the best. As a publisher of the Greater Than a Tourist, as well as the popular *50 Things to Know* book series, we strive to help you learn about new places, spark your imagination, and inspire you. Wherever you are and whatever you do I wish you safe, fun, and inspiring travel.

Lisa Rusczyk Ed. D.
CZYK Publishing

>TOURIST

```
WELCOME TO
> TOURIST
```

>TOURIST

Clifton beach - a popular area for locals and visitors alike

Clifton 4th Beach

11

A panoramic view over the Victoria Basin at the V&A Waterfront

Greater Cape Town

>TOURIST

"Travel is fatal to prejudice, bigotry, and narrow mindedness, and many of our people need it sorely on these accounts. Broad, wholesome, charitable views of men and things cannot be acquired by vegetating in one little corner of earth all one's lifetime."

– Mark Twain

Cape Town. Our home, the "mother city" of South Africa, is one of the most beautiful places on Earth. As a tour operator and local tour guide, I've been guiding groups and individuals around Cape Town and the Cape Peninsula and creating itineraries for international travellers for more than twenty years. With Table Mountain and the Atlantic Ocean on our doorstep, Cape Town has so much to do, so much to taste and so many hidden gems to explore. One of our family's favourite pastimes is traveling around our own city and exploring these hidden gems. We take a pencil and spin it, and go in the direction that it points, because there is something to enjoy in every part of this amazing place. We hike the mountains, run the trails, and kayak or swim the waters. We explore the markets, museums, and galleries. We visit the artisan roasters, brewers and locally-owned restaurants. In the next 50 tips, I will share my local experience with you so that you can make the most out of your visit to Cape Town.

Cape Town
South Africa

Cape Town South Africa Climate

	High	Low
January	83	63
February	84	63
March	81	61
April	77	59
May	72	56
June	68	53
July	68	52
August	68	53
September	70	55
October	76	58
November	78	59
December	81	62

GreaterThanaTourist.com

Temperatures are in Fahrenheit degrees.
Source: NOAA

>TOURIST

1. SPEND TIME

It is common for visitors to book a three-day, two-night stay in Cape Town. I can promise you that this is not enough time. Do yourself a favour and plan to stay for a week or longer in Cape Town. Or to go even further, Cape Town is emerging as a popular "digital nomad" destination. With world-class infrastructure and a currency (Rand) that is massively undervalued to the Dollar or Euro, many visitors stay in the Cape Town area for several months of the year. If you have the opportunity in life, Cape Town is a great place to rent an apartment for a few months and really get to know the culture and the place. This would truly make you "greater than a tourist".

2. BE A RESPONSIBLE TRAVELLER

I love Cape Town and want to preserve this beautiful environment for many future generations of locals and visitors alike. Please make responsible choices when traveling by:

- Saving water and electricity. Cape Town and the Western Cape, although green and lush, does experience periodic droughts and shortages in electricity. Please use water and electricity sparingly.

- Protect and support local communities and businesses. You can have a positive economic effect on the people of South Africa by supporting small, local, family-run businesses. Book your tour, accommodation and activity directly to save these businesses from paying high commissions to third party agents, often located thousands of kilometres away in Europe or America.
- Reduce, reuse and recycle. Please make use of the ample recycling facilities in and around our beautiful city. You can bring your own water bottle (water is safe to drink); reusable coffee mug and reusable shopping bag to reduce single use materials.

>TOURIST

3. BE SAFE

Cape Town and the areas you will visit as a tourist are generally "safe", but like in other cities around the world, you have to take precautions to make sure you are not a victim of petty crime. Follow these safety tips:

• Never walk alone at night. Rather use an Uber or taxi, which are readily available. (We will discuss getting around in Cape Town a few points down.)

• Do not look like a typical tourist; make an effort to blend in with the locals. Use a small backpack or handbag for your belongings, and ditch the floppy tourist hat, hiking boots and safari gear.

• When withdrawing cash, make use of an ATM that is well-lit and in a busy area, such as a shopping mall. Be aware of any person standing around the ATM. Never carry big amounts of cash with you.

4. USE LOCAL CURRENCY

In South Africa we use South African Rand (ZAR). Foreign currencies are not widely accepted. This is 2021, please ditch the traveller's cheques and leave your local currency at home. You can exchange USD, GBP or Euros at local banks, but the commissions are high. Cheques are not accepted in South Africa. I would recommend the following methods of payment:

- Snapscan and Zapper. These handy mobile apps are very popular and used all around the city in restaurants, for parking at food markets and even at street vendors. These are very simple to use. Download the app on your smartphone, load your debit or credit card (foreign or local) and scan the vendor's QR code when you need to make payment.
- Cash is king? Not really anymore in South Africa. Cash is mostly accepted, but some shops, restaurants and markets do not accept cash anymore. It is however always wise to have some cash on you. ATMs are widely available and a more affordable and less time-consuming way of getting cash than exchanging foreign currency.
- Bring your local debit and credit cards, they are widely accepted. Let your bank know you are

>TOURIST

traveling to South Africa, and make sure you have a way to receive an OTP (one time pin) or other method of verifying transactions. Please leave your Diner's Club card at home; we know you get many rewards, but local small businesses pay big fees for swiping these cards. Many establishments will not accept Diner's Club for that reason.

5. GET AROUND CAPE TOWN EASILY

Public transport in Cape Town, such as trains and minibus taxis, are generally a mode of travel that is best left to locals. Minibus taxis are a cultural phenomenon all their own, you will know one when you see a van loaded with 16 or more people, blaring music and using hand gestures you can't decipher! Although this looks like lots of fun, this is generally not a safe way to travel for foreigners. For a city break I also would not recommend that you rent a car, as traffic in Cape Town can be quite bad during events and during rush hour and parking is limited. I would recommend you use the following modes of transport:

• My Citi bus service. This is a relatively new bus transport system in Cape Town. Once you understand the routes and card system it is an easy, safe and affordable way of getting around. There are stations all over the city and suburbs where you can purchase travel cards. This does however take a bit longer than private options.

- Local tour operator. There are many great and reliable tour operators in Cape Town. Book your airport transfer and day tours before you arrive in Cape Town and a professional driver who is also your guide will pick you up from the airport and share all that Cape Town has to offer.
- Taxi Service or Uber. Metered taxis and Ubers are widely available around Cape Town. Please ask your host, guest house or hotel reception to give you the name and number of a reliable taxi driver.

6. CHOOSE GREAT ACCOMMODATION

We are absolutely spoiled when it comes to accommodation in Cape Town. We have great hotels, guest houses, backpackers/hostels and self-catering apartments such as Airbnb. The most difficult choice is to decide between great mountain views or great ocean views. There is something for every traveller.

>TOURIST

Pro tip: Book your accommodation directly with the establishment or tour operator. These small businesses pay huge commissions to big international booking websites. By booking directly, your money reaches the establishment in South Africa, and you can make a positive local economic impact during your stay. Furthermore, by choosing to book something smaller and owner-run, you get so much more than just accommodation. You also get to experience local hospitality, something you do not want to miss out on when you travel, especially to South Africa. For longer stays having an apartment with your own kitchen is ideal, but there will be much less interaction with the locals. Many small guest houses and hostels are owner-run and managed and it is great to meet the people instead of just being a number at a big chain hotel. Guest houses are a popular accommodation type in South Africa which is similar to what Americans would call a "bed and breakfast". Talk to the owners/managers/staff in these places about what they recommend, where to eat, what to do, and what to experience in the city. Tips from locals are the best.

My favourite guest house:

- Parker Cottage: Fairtrade accredited and owner-run with great views of Table Mountain. Parker Cottage is located within walking distance of the city centre as well as many attractions and restaurants. You will experience living in a historic South African home in a residential neighbourhood.

My favourite backpackers/hostels:

- Atlantic Point Backpackers, Green Point: Small owner-run establishment. Very clean, tidy and well-run. They offer so much to do for the guests, it is the perfect place for a solo traveller to meet other likeminded travellers. Don't miss braai night. (You will learn all about braai in one of my tips below.)
- BIG Backpackers, Green Point: Charming and small owner-run backpackers. Green Point is short walk from many good restaurants, shops and the promenade.
- Once in Cape Town. Not a small backpacker like the others on my list, but probably the hippest place to be. This Fairtrade accredited establishment is on the bustling Kloof Street, where all the "cool kids" hang out. They serve excellent coffee and have a great bar.

>TOURIST

7. BRING SOMETHING WARM

This travel tip is probably in every guide book and something experienced travellers know well, but in Cape Town it is particularly important. Pack for 4 seasons. With the nearby mountains, ocean and sea currents, weather is difficult to predict and can be different in localized parts of Cape Town. It often happens that the weather forecast says it will be a beautiful day, we go out and hike somewhere, and then the weather quickly changes for the worse, leaving us wishing for a jacket. The same is true the other way around: you wake up to a foggy and cool morning, get out your jacket, trousers and boots, and head out for the day. Around 10 am the fog lifts or you drive to the other side of the mountain and then it's a beautiful clear day and you are stuck in winter gear. Always pack those sandals and shorts AND a jacket and cap. I also never travel anywhere around Cape Town without a towel and my board shorts in case I come across a great river, rock pool, or dam to have a quick dip in.

8. TAKE AN ORIENTATION TOUR

Start with an introduction to the City tour on day 1 or 2 of your stay. Tour guides will point out where to go, where not to go, what to eat and tell you a few of their secrets of the city. Although this is "touristy", it is a great way of getting an orientation to a new destination. There are several ways of doing this, I would recommend three:

- Do a guided tour with my company, Earthstompers Adventures, or Cape Food & Wine Tours. Your guide will pick you up from your accommodation's doorstep and drive you around the city to point out all the places of interest, take you to the top of Table Mountain, or even explore the trendy suburb of Woodstock with you. The benefit of hiring a private vehicle/guide is to take the hassle out of getting around, fitting a lot of attractions or activities in a small amount of time, and allowing the guide to customize the tour to your interests and tastes.
- Do a "free" walking tour. These shorter tours depart from various spots around the city. There is no fixed price for these tours; you basically just pay by giving a tip. I would recommend Free Walking Tours Cape Town (look for the green umbrellas).

>TOURIST

- Go Topless. The red open-top hop-on, hop-off bus is a great and affordable way of getting an orientation to Cape Town. The on-board commentary is clear, informative, and offered in multiple languages. If you only have one day, I would recommend taking this bus and "hopping off" at points that interest you.

9. CHECK THE WIND BEFORE CHOOSING YOUR BEACH

Two things you will definitely experience when you travel to Cape Town is wind and a beach. Nobody likes to go to a beach when it is windy, but luckily in Cape Town we have a beach for every wind direction. Table Mountain acts as a superb wind barrier. During summer months we have a south-easterly wind, also known as the "Cape Doctor" because it blows all the air pollution away from the city and out to the ocean. Some days this wind can be very strong and a visit to beaches on the False Bay coast is not pleasant (except if you are up for getting sandblasted). On these days rather visit the protected beaches of Clifton, Camps Bay or Llandudno.

During autumn, spring and winter we have the north-western wind blowing. These days it is best to visit the beaches on the False Bay coast such as Muizenberg, Fish Hoek or Simons Town.

10. HIKE TABLE MOUNTAIN

A visit to Cape Town is not complete without visiting one of the seven wonders of nature, the iconic Table Mountain. There are two ways of getting to the top: hiking or taking the cable car. The cable car operates seven days a week, weather dependent. Go early, the cable car gets quite busy late in the day. It is possible to book your tickets for the cable car online in advance, but know that the cable car can close in inclement weather. Refunds for tickets purchased online are relatively straightforward.

I personally recommend hiking up Table Mountain if you have the time and fitness. There are more than 100 hiking trails going up Table Mountain; go with a local or with a guide when you attempt any of these hikes. Two excellent hiking guides are Binny Ridgeway of Ridgway Ramblers and Stuart Coffey of Wild Things Outdoor.

>TOURIST

When I visit the mountain, I like to hike up and take the cable car down (one way cable car tickets are available). Three of my favourite hiking routes are:

- Platteklip Gorge. This is the easiest and fastest way to the top. The trail starts about one kilometre east of the lower cable car station, and takes only 1.5 to 3 hours (one way) depending on your fitness. As this is the quickest hike, there is likely to be a lot of foot traffic. A moderate level of fitness is necessary to take the big steps up on the boulders of Table Mountain.
- Kasteelpoort. This is a 2-to-4-hour one-way hike starting in Camps Bay. The views over the Twelve Apostles and Camps Bay are magnificent, and this is a less congested trail.
- Skeleton Gorge. This is a 2-to-4-hour hike that takes you through the forest from Kirstenbosch Botanical Gardens.

Pro tips for visiting Table Mountain:

- Go early, as visiting Table Mountain is weather dependent. The cable way is closed and hiking is not recommended in case of strong winds and low visibility. The cable car website is regularly updated on weather conditions at the top of the mountain and whether the cable car is operating.

- Plan to visit Table Mountain on the first day of your Cape Town itinerary. If the weather is good on day one, go for it; if the weather doesn't cooperate, then you still have time to make it to the top of the mountain later in your stay.
- Always take a rain jacket and something warm; the weather can change quickly.
- Hydrate. Many people underestimate our mountain; please drink enough water. Food and drinks are available at the restaurant on top of the mountain, but if you hike up, be sure to take enough water.
- Never walk alone, and take note of the emergency number should you need assistance.

11. SEE SUNRISE OR SUNSET ON LION'S HEAD

Another favourite for Capetonians is seeing the sun set in the West and then the moon rise in the East from the top of Lions Head. This is a relatively easy hike which requires medium fitness and some tolerance for heights. Your reward at the top is a beautiful 360-degree view all around the city, stretching from Camps Bay, Table Mountain, to the

>TOURIST

Helderberg Mountains in the distance. I would also recommend going with a guide and going late afternoon for sunset or very early for sunrise. During a full moon the hike is very busy; allow extra time to get to the top. Take a headlamp, a jacket, and plenty of water. Pro tip: pack a picnic to enjoy the top!

12. VISIT THE PENGUINS

The African penguin is a somewhat unexpected resident of Cape Town's shores. Visit the endangered African penguin colony in Simons Town. Take your swimming costume - you can swim at Boulders Beach, and you might even be lucky enough to be able to swim close to the penguins! Use the smaller entrance of the two entrances to get to the beach or ask one of the staff where the swimming beach is.

13. VOLUNTEER

I'm never sure who gets more out of volunteering: the volunteer or the person they are trying to help. Either way, volunteering is a good way to get a real look at how locals live, and make a positive contribution to people in need. A reputable local company to arrange local volunteering is the SAVE Foundation. They support projects ranging from early education to medical services to community feeding schemes. Even if you don't volunteer in person, consider making a donation to a cause that touches your heart.

14. GO TO THE FURTHEST SOUTHWESTERN POINT ON THE AFRICAN CONTINENT

Taking a tour down to the Cape of Good Hope National Park is a worthwhile day trip. I would recommend booking a day tour with a tour operator like Earthstompers Adventures, or using the topless red bus city tour. This trip takes a full day to do properly, traveling along the beautiful Twelve Apostles, Hout Bay, and Chapmans Peak, to the National Park; the return journey goes along the False Bay coast past Simons Town, Fish Hoek and Muizenberg. You can add a visit to the penguins at Boulders Beach, a visit to a winery in the Constantia wine valley or a visit to Kirstenbosch Botanical Gardens on a day trip around the Peninsula.

>TOURIST

In summer I would suggest you go early to avoid long lines entering the park. Leave enough time to walk to the two light houses (about 45 minutes return from the main parking area) and Cape of Good Hope when you visit the park.

15. VISIT ROBBEN ISLAND

This historic island, just off the Cape Town coast, has a long and somewhat notorious history. If you are into politics, history, or social justice, it is worth a visit. The tour takes about three hours and starts with a 30 to 40-minute ferry crossing to Robben Island from the V&A Waterfront with stunning views of the city and Table Bay. On arrival, you will join a short bus tour of the island and then visit the prison and cell where Nelson Mandela was detained. Tours are conducted by former political prisoners, who are able to give first hand context to the volatile apartheid years in South Africa's history.

Unfortunately, Robben Island is not very well managed from an administrative perspective; a three-hour tour can easily turn into four or five hours and ferries do not always run on time. It is wise to give yourself extra time both before and after your scheduled time and not make firm plans for after the trip. Time slots and tickets are limited, so book your tickets online in advance if visiting Robben Island is a priority for your time in Cape Town.

16. VISIT A LOCAL BREWERY

The global trend of craft brewing is hot in Cape Town. Visit one of the hip local craft breweries, all of which offer tastings and some of which offer tours. My favourites are Devils Peak Taproom in Salt River and Woodstock Brewery in the Woodstock neighbourhood. If you visit the winelands, make a stop at Cape Town Brewing Company on the Spice Route wine estate.

17. VISIT A COFFEE ROASTER

Cape Town is definitely a place for coffee lovers. I would recommend Truth, Origin and Rosetta Coffee Roasters for your caffeine kick. These coffee roasters are all in the city centre and form a big part of Cape Town's creative culinary scene. Coffee roasteries have become some of the trendiest spots to hang out, grab a breakfast, or catch up on some work. I have travelled to many different countries, and I always marvel at how spoiled I am by Cape Town's coffee.

18. TAKE A FOODIE TOUR

I feel that one of the best ways to get to know a country is through its food, and Cape Town has incredible diversity and quality. So many flavours, colours and textures representing South Africa's rainbow nation and influences from around the world. If you love food & wine but find the whole scene a bit overwhelming, join a foodie tour. This is a great introduction that will show you some of the unique tastes of the area, and help you plan to make the most of the food & drink options while you are in Cape Town. Cape Food & Wine or Cape Fusion offers great one-day walking foodie tours of Cape Town, which visit small owner-run businesses and artisans around the city. Joining a foodie tour allows you to experience food that is delicious, typical to South Africa, and most importantly food with a story. The guides are all "foodies", and will be excited to share their favourite discoveries with you.

19. VISIT A WINERY (OR TEN)

The wines of the Western Cape are some of the best you will ever taste, at a fraction of European or American prices. The winelands scenery is out of this world: beautiful mountains, rolling hills, and indigenous fynbos vegetation. The wine farms are visitor friendly with well-manicured gardens and beautiful architecture, both old and new. Most of the farms offer wine tastings, restaurants, delis and many offer guided cellar tours.

I would always recommend a visit to the "classic" Cape Winelands (Stellenbosch, Franschhoek and Paarl) as the main wine region. Perhaps even more spectacular but further away from Cape Town is the Elgin Valley, the Hemel-and-Aarde (Heaven-and-Earth) Wine Valley, the West Coast and Swartland wine areas; to visit these areas that are a little further afield, it is best to book a private tour.

If you are really pressed for time, two wine regions are located within a 15-minute drive from Cape Town:
- Durbanville Hills. Durbanville is known for white wine, particularly Sauvignon Blanc. I would

>TOURIST

recommend a visit to Diemersdal Winery, De Grendel Winery and Durbanville Hills.

- Constantia. In the oldest wine region in South Africa, I would recommend a visit to the oldest winery in South Africa, Groot Constantia; as well as stops at Constantia Glen and Steenberg.

It should go without saying that it's best not to drive yourself on a wine tour! For safety and enjoyment, book a scheduled wine tour with a company like Wine Flies or a customized private wine tour with Cape Food & Wine. Not only will you have transportation, but you will find that the tour guide is an enthusiastic and knowledgeable wine drinker, who can take you to some of their favourite wineries.

Lunch in the winelands is a must; chat to the local tour operator to arrange anything from a picnic lunch to a seven-course fine dining experience. It is difficult for me to pick a favourite, but if I had to choose one place to dine in the winelands it would probably be Werf restaurant on Boschendal wine farm. Werf focuses on "farm-to-table" dining, with a magnificent vegetable garden and their own herd of black Angus cattle. The food is both exceptional and well-priced. If you choose to pair your meal with Boschendal's exceptional wine, plan to spend at least three hours there!

20. BRAAI

Do not leave our country before you have a braai. Braai is a South African version of barbeque, but on open flames, not gas or coals. I feel that the word "barbecue" does not do justice to the way that we South Africans roast meat on the open fire. The word barbeque doesn't capture the larger cultural significance of a braai. In South Africa people braai when they are sad; braai when they are happy; braai when they celebrate something; basically, any excuse to light a fire with friends and family. With a braai there is delicious food, but the experience is about more than the food or method of preparation; it is about the comradery of standing around the fire, drink in hand and chatting the night away.

Many game lodges in South Africa would offer a "braai" evening, which would be a lot of fun. But it does not quite capture the experience of a real braai at a real home. For that reason, my wife and I have begun offering braais for some of our Earthstompers clients. Come to our house, let us pour you a glass of wine, and join us around the fire. You can relax and watch us prepare the food if you like, or we welcome you to get hands on and help us for an interactive cooking experience. We offer starters/snacks, a main meal with several kinds of meat or fish and vegetable sides, and a dessert. Each course is paired with local wines from the region, perhaps even from the wineries you visited if you joined us on a wine tour that day. For those hard-core foodies, you can even join me earlier in the day to source the fresh produce, meat or fish, and wine for the evening's braai from sustainable producers around Cape Town.

21. WALK BREE STREET & ENJOY FIRST THURSDAYS

During your time in Cape Town, you will eventually wonder down Bree Street, our famous foodie street. Take your time and wander into the shops, restaurants and galleries. Have a glass of wine and a cheese or charcuterie platter at a wine bar, taste a chocolate truffle at Honest Chocolate, get a croissant at Jason's Bakery or enjoy a tapas-style lunch at Chefs Warehouse. Finish the day by joining the locals for a cocktail and live entertainment at La Parada, one of Cape Town's favourite hangouts for after work drinks and snacks.

If you visit Cape Town on the first Thursday of the month, make sure to put some time aside for First Thursdays. Galleries and restaurants stay open late, and they close portions of the Bree Street to allow for pedestrians. Many live shows and art exhibitions are on offer as well as amazing food. This is where you can get a true local vibe.

>TOURIST

22. SEEK OUT THE FRESH SEAFOOD

Cape Town is surrounded by the plankton-rich, cold Atlantic Ocean, and the warm Indian Ocean is not far away. This makes for an abundance of excellent fresh seafood! Sample live mussels, crayfish, oysters and fresh fish at:

- Kalky's Fish & Chips on Kalk Bay Harbour. Kalky's offers classic fried fish and chips. The fish would traditionally be hake, a moist, soft flaky fish. This is definitely the locals' choice, and the queue can be long!

- Seabreeze Fish & Shell. This popular seafood restaurant at the top of Bree Street is a stylish must for seafood lovers. Look out for multiple happy hours daily, when oysters and bubbly are half price!

- Willoughby and Co. A sushi lover's dream, located at a bit of an odd location inside the mall at the V&A Waterfront. If I voluntarily go to into the mall for a restaurant, you know it must be good!

23. PLAN A FINE DINING EVENING IN CAPE TOWN

For those who watch the top restaurants lists, plan FAR ahead for your time in Cape Town. There are many great fine dining options, but if you would like to get into the top restaurants, you have to make reservations early…like sometimes 6 months to a year ahead of time. If you are not into fine dining or haven't ever experienced it, Cape Town might be a great chance to plan a special evening. The Rand is likely to be weak against your home currency, so fine dining for tourists is actually relatively affordable. Three of my favourites:

- Test Kitchen. Book very early for a spot at Luke Dale Robert's famous restaurant. Enjoy 4 - 10 course food & wine pairing lunches and dinners, located at the historic Biscuit Mill in Woodstock. A regular on the top 10 South African restaurant lists, the Test Kitchen is at the top of many foodies' bucket lists.

- La Colombe in the Southern suburbs. Great views, great service an experience not to be missed. A regular on the list of the top 50 restaurants around the world.

>TOURIST

- Chefs Warehouse at Beau-Constantia or city bowl. Run by Liam Tomlin, a culinary legend in Cape Town, Chefs Warehouse focuses on small plate, tapas-style meals paired with great local wines. Probably my favourite when it comes to fine dining, because it is innovative and special but also casual and doesn't feel pretentious.

24. VISIT A LOCAL FARMERS MARKET

We have many great markets in Cape Town, because we have so many great local artisans, farmers and creative people who call this home. Artisans you will find here are small organic farmers, butchers, cheese makers, pasta makers, charcuterie makers, and craft beer brewers. My favourite markets around the city are:

- Oranjezicht City Farm Market. Great location close to the V&A Waterfront, with shopping, food stands, live entertainment and amazing produce. We love to go on a Saturday morning after a run on the promenade at Green Point. We grab a coffee, a breakfast/brunch and then do our weekly shopping from the local vendors, getting awesome produce, and exceptional meat and seafood products. Many days we can just not leave and end up staying for drinks and live entertainment. This market is only open on Saturdays and Sundays; sometimes during season, they open Wednesday and Friday evenings also.

- Old Biscuit Mill. One of the original markets, located in Woodstock. Popular amongst locals and tourists alike for great food options and vibe. It usually ends up being a big party when the music starts and the wines and beers start to flow. This is a great market, but the only down side is the crowds – go early if you want to avoid them.

25. DEVOUR A STEAK

If you like meat, you have come to the right country. With wide open spaces, South Africa has some amazing free-range and grass-fed beef. Butchers have become so skilled at maturing their steaks for the best flavour and tenderness. A steakhouse that has stood the test of time is Nelsons Eye. Excellent meats, perfectly prepared in an old school restaurant that has not changed much since they opened in the early 1960s. Be sure to make a reservation in advance, as they can get busy any time of the week. You can also try The Butcher Shop &

>TOURIST

Grill in Mouille Point, or the Hussar Grill. Hussar is a chain restaurant, which I would normally avoid, but each location manages to have high quality, excellent steak, and a comfortable steakhouse atmosphere.

If you have the opportunity to grill (braai) your own steak while you are in Cape Town, head to Frankie Fenner Meat Merchants, who call themselves "Cape Town's ethical butchery".

26. GRAB A BURGER

From the usual old school burgers to gourmet burgers, veggie burgers and no-bun burgers, Cape Town has it all. A few places not to miss:
- Clarke's Bar and Dining. On the trendy Bree street, great on-street vibe.
- Dogs Bollocks. No frills, exceptional burgers. No cutlery, waiters or fancy manners, just excellent food.
- Redemption Burgers. This hugely popular burger spot at the Old Biscuit Mill is probably my favourite. It does not have to stand back from its neighbours that are two of South Africa's top fine dining restaurants; the food here is amazing.

27. JUMP OUT OF A PLANE

No better view than seeing Table Mountain and Table Bay from 10 000 feet; no better adrenaline boost than to jump from a perfectly good plane in a tandem skydive! Book with Skydive Cape Town, located about 40 minutes' drive from the city centre, or Mother City Skydiving, located about a one-hour drive from the city. You can also get your local tour operator to arrange this activity and transport as part of an organized tour. Pro Tip: Combine skydiving with a Winelands day tour. This way you can experience an early morning sky dive en route to taste some amazing wines in the afternoon.

>TOURIST

28. MEET THE "MARINE BIG 5" OR DIVE WITH SHARKS

Experience the abundance of marine life on our shores with shark, whale and marine "Big 5" trips around Dyer Island. (The marine Big 5 are whale, shark, seal, penguin and dolphin.) The Dyer Island ecosystem is a special place where you can see African penguins, three different dolphin species, three different whale species, two different shark species, and up to forty thousand cape fur seals, depending on your luck for the day.

Join Dyer Island Cruises or Marine Dynamics for these outings – they are simply the best of the companies operating in the area, and make a major contribution to marine research. They have an on-board marine biologist on every boat that will entertain and educate you on all the species you see in this amazing ecosystem.

The trips depart from Gansbaai, which is about 2.5 hours east of Cape Town. Marine Dynamics and Dyer Island Cruises offer daily pickups and drop offs in the Cape Town city centre, so you can enjoy a stress-free day trip.

29. PARAGLIDE OFF LIONS HEAD OR SIGNAL HILL

People from all over the world come to Cape Town to paraglide. You do not need any specialized experience to do a tandem paraglide; your tandem instructor will take care of the important parts so that you can marvel at the beautiful views over Clifton, Camps Bay, Table Mountain, Robben Island and Table Bay. Pro Tip: Go early; you need near perfect weather conditions for paragliding. On a windy day, the wind usually comes up later in the day.

30. SOAR THROUGH THE MOUNTAINS AT CAPE CANOPY TOUR

An hour outside of Cape Town in the Elgin Valley is the Hottentots-Holland Nature Reserve, where you can zipline high up in this World Heritage Site. Soar over valleys and waterfalls, ziplining along a series of steel cables up to 330m long. There are plenty of ziplines in the world, but there are none with more beautiful scenery. A dream day out for me would be to do the canopy tour in the morning, and a food & wine tour of the Elgin Valley in the afternoon.

>TOURIST

31. CATCH A BIG ONE

Catching a yellowfin tuna in the deep sea off of Cape Point is one of my best life experiences. You can choose to catch and release, or keep your monster for the pan or the braai after your outing. This day tour was always on my bucket list, and after I went my first time I kept going back for more. No prior experience is required; they have all the equipment on board and will tell you exactly what to do when you get a tuna on the line.

The boat trip takes you from Simons Town or Hout Bay harbour, traveling about 1.5 to 2 hours southwest out to sea where you meet the warmer sea currents. You will then put the lines out and wait until the reel sings, then it is a battle between you and your fish! I would recommend a trip with the passionate crew of Fish Tales Charters; they take great care of you and would surely put you onto a big one. Pro Tip: If you are prone to sea sickness, this outing is not for you. You will be out at sea all day, and most of the day you will not be able to see land.

32. SWIM WITH THE SEALS

Meet the furry locals from Hout Bay, the Cape fur seals. These playful creatures have been entertaining people in the harbour for many years, stealing the fish offcuts from the harbour market. The best experience is to see them in their natural environment, the cool Atlantic Ocean. I would recommend a seal snorkelling experience with Animal Ocean Seal Snorkelling, who operates from Hout Bay. You will enjoy a short boat ride from Hout Bay to Duiker Island within the Karbonkelberg marine protected area, where you will find a seal colony of about 5000 Cape fur seals. Enjoy a snorkel with the inquisitive seals in their natural environment. You will spend about 45 minutes to 1 hour in the water with the seals. Give yourself about 2.5 hours for the whole experience. All equipment is provided.

33. LEARN TO SURF

If you are an experienced surfer, you will find good waves in Cape Town year-round. Even if you have never surfed before, Cape Town is a great place to take a surfing lesson and see the beauty of our city from the ocean. Mountains are your backdrop at most of our white sandy beaches where you'll also find some great cafes to enjoy a post-surf 'chow'. Located on a peninsula, we have the option to surf two different coastlines depending on wind and swell direction which is why mobility is key to ensure you're getting to the best waves on the day. Join Stoked Surf for your Cape Town surf experience. They provide a knowledgeable surf instructor, wetsuits and surf boards. The also do pickups from anywhere in the city centre. No experience required for a surf lesson, just some balance and moderate fitness. If you already know how to surf, Stoked can also rent you a surf board and a wetsuit for a day out in the waves.

34. LISTEN TO A SUNSET CONCERT IN KIRSTENBOSCH BOTANICAL GARDENS

Every summer Kirstenbosch Botanical Gardens offers a series of concerts by local and international artists in the beautiful setting at the foot of Table Mountain. Bring a picnic basket, bring great wine and enjoy the sunset while you dance into the night. Pro Tip: Go online and look at the concert schedule before you arrive in Cape Town, and book tickets early. Arrive well before the concert begins; the gardens are beautiful and worth a walk around before the show. These shows usually book out and space is limited, so arrive early to get a great view of the stage and a place in the shade, as the sun is quite warm just before sunset.

35. WATCH A RUGBY MATCH AT CAPE TOWN STADIUM

Cape Town is home to The Stormers and Western Province rugby team. No better way to experience real Cape Town "gees" (local word for amazing vibe) than to attend one of these rugby matches. South Africans love rugby so there will be some great people watching and of course a rugby match. The local team is pretty good and would get the crowd on their feet quickly. Pro tip: Enjoy a boerewors roll (a South African style hotdog with a spicy meat sausage) from one of the local vendors.

>TOURIST

36. GO FOR A RUN, WALK OR CYCLE ON THE PROMENADE

During early mornings, the promenade at Sea Point is a hive of locals walking their dogs, running, and enjoying the fresh sea air and great views. The promenade is nice and flat, making for a great running spot. The views towards Table Mountain and Robben Island are beautiful, and this is a great place to get a sense of city life.

37. ABSEIL TABLE MOUNTAIN

This is certainly a different way of experiencing one of the seven natural wonders of nature, Table Mountain. The views from the top of Table Mountain are great, but from the sheer cliff a thousand meters above sea level on the side of Table Mountain where you abseil it is even better. (If you dare to look!) You will have spectacular views over the Atlantic seaboard, Twelve Apostles, Lion's Head and Camps Bay far below.

38. GO FOR HIGH TEA

Although South Africa has moved on from British rule, the British influence is still visible around Cape Town. One of the traditions that is here to stay is high tea, a popular ritual amongst locals and tourists. There are many great high tea options, but probably the best and oldest version is high tea at the Mount Nelson Hotel in the Gardens neighbourhood of Cape Town. Join them for an indulgent feast in their bright and sunny lounge. Think tea, pastries, cakes, sandwiches all stacked on tiers with live piano music at this beautiful hotel. Pro tip: You don't have to drink tea. Local craft gin is also frequently enjoyed!

39. TAKE A COOKING CLASS IN THE BO KAAP

Enjoy an educational cooking and cultural afternoon with great traditional food and great company in the colourful Bo-Kaap. I would recommend visiting Faeeza's home kitchen. This is really Faeeza's home and not a tourist restaurant. Faeeza and her daughters offer a culinary experience in their home where you will not only learn how to cook Cape Malay dishes, but also learn about Cape

>TOURIST

Malay culture and traditions. If you are lucky enough, you could also meet the grandkids. You will leave the Bo Kaap with a full stomach and heart.

40. SEE CONTEMPORARY AFRICAN ART

Zeitz Museum of Contemporary Art Africa (Zeitz MOCAA) is a relatively new non-profit public museum of art, opened in 2017. In a great example of historic building reuse, the museum is housed in a renovated 1921 Grain Silo at the V&A Waterfront. The museum houses the world's largest collection of contemporary African art. The museum's mission is to exhibit, collect, and preserve contemporary art from Africa and its diaspora, and to offer educational programs to encourage intercultural understanding of art and artists in an African context. Pro tip: there are nine floors of art to see, so give yourself plenty of time – perhaps even a full day for art lovers.

41. LEARN ABOUT SOUTH AFRICA'S DIVERSE CULTURES AND HISTORY

From the indigenous San people to the Dutch and British colonists, Cape Town has an interesting and important place in world history. Luckily, there are many local museums and historical displays where you can learn about it. A great place to start is in the Company's Gardens, where the Dutch East India Company established a stopover supply station to get fresh vegetables and water when ships travelled from Europe to the Far East. From there, visit the Cape Town Castle, built by the Company between 1666 and 1679 whilst tensions with the British were heating up. In more recent history, the District 6 Museum documents this thriving multi-cultural community which was declared a "whites only" area by the apartheid government, and subsequently bulldozed in the 1970s.

>TOURIST

42. HEAR THE NOON GUN ON SIGNAL HILL

Experience one of Cape Town's oldest traditions, the firing of the Noon Gun cannon at the South African Navy's Lion Battery on Signal Hill. Every day at 12:00 noon, they load two cannons; the second in case the first one does not fire. For Capetonians the sound of the cannon fire is a daily occurrence and a quick double check on the watch that it is indeed 12:00; but some tourists and pigeons inevitably get startled every day at noon when they hear the canon shot! Pro Tip: arrive early, about 11:30. A brief history will be told while cannons are being loaded, a flag will be lifted and cannon will be fired at exactly 12:00. Use ear plugs, the bang is very loud.

43. VISIT KALK BAY

Visit this little gem of a coastal town on the False Bay coast about 30 minutes south of Cape Town. This small town is filled with interesting shops, restaurants, antiques and a lovely harbour. I would highly recommend a stop in the harbour to experience the vibrant fish market and meet the local seal colony. On a sunny day I would recommend a swim in the tidal pool or some time on the colourful St James beach. A beer and fish & chips at the Brass Bell is a must.

44. WATCH THE SUNSET FROM THE OCEAN

Sunsets are always special, and even more dazzling from the water. Take time and enjoy the sunset from a boat or a yacht with a drink in hand and breath-taking views. Cruises depart from the V&A Waterfront and are about 1.5 – 3 hours long, depending on what options you select. Weather depending, you would sail around Sea Point, Mouille Point and anchor for sunset close to Clifton beach. Imagine the picture, once you move away from land the views you would have: Robben Island, Table Mountain, Twelve Apostles with Clifton and Camps Bay Beaches! So many great views and landmarks in one picture. This is your Instagram moment.

>TOURIST

45. SHOP LOCAL

I'm not a big shopper myself, but many tourists wish to take home a special item from their time in Cape Town. As mentioned elsewhere, the most positive impact you can make with your money is buying from local vendors. Watch out for the kitschy "African" art and souvenirs; whilst the little wooden elephants or safari-themed prints might catch your eye, many of these items are not made in South Africa, or in Africa at all. The best places to shop for legit crafts, art, jewellery and souvenirs are the local farmers markets (mentioned in tip 24), Woodstock (mentioned in tip 49), and the Watershed at the V&A Waterfront. The Watershed in particular hosts an impressive array of clothing, art, ceramics, textiles, and furniture, and you can be confident that these items are locally produced.

46. ENJOY SUNDOWNERS ON A ROOFTOP

Locals love to enjoy drinks, love great views and love being outdoors. What to do in a city centre with many high-rise buildings? Rooftop bars are the answer and there are many amazing rooftop bars and restaurants in Cape Town. My favourites are Sky Bar at Grand Daddy Hotel, Tjing Tjing Rooftop and Gorgeous George.

47. SUP AROUND THE V&A WATERFRONT

Go for a SUP (stand-up paddleboard) on the canals at the V&A Waterfront. It is a great way to get out, get wet and get active. No need to do a guided tour here; you can rent your SUP for 30 minutes to 1.5 hours and enjoy the scenes of the V&A Waterfront channels from the water. No experience is required, although good balance and moderate fitness helps. They do offer a quick briefing and lesson for first timers.

48. FLY THROUGH THE SKY

The mountains, Robben Island and the Peninsula are spectacular to see, but even more awe-inspiring from the sky. Cape Town has many scenic helicopter flight options ranging from 10 minutes to 1.5 hours. With the Table Mountain situated right in the middle of the city, it can be difficult to understand the city

>TOURIST

layout whilst in a car or on foot; but from the helicopter you get to see the whole picture of the mountain in the middle, Cape Point stretching to the south, Robben Island, False Bay and Table Bay. Contact Cape Town Helicopters; they operate from the V&A Waterfront. Pro tip: if budget allows, take a trip to the winelands by helicopter! Enjoy wine tastings and lunch, flying there and back.

49. VISIT WOODSTOCK

This trendy and creative neighbourhood of Cape Town is only a few minutes by bus or Uber from the city centre. Woodstock is a hub for many young entrepreneurs, artisans, innovative media, artists, foodies, and designers.

Many of the foodie attractions I mention in my earlier tips are located in Woodstock. (Biscuit Mill Market, Revolution Burger Bar, Test Kitchen, Woodstock Brewing Company and Devils Peak Tap Room.) Take this into consideration when you plan an outing to Woodstock.

Many buildings in Woodstock are covered with murals, and it is special to see how this art enlivens the neighbourhood that used to be run down a few years ago. I would highly recommend a street art tour street of Woodstock with Juma Art Tours. You will not only learn about the interesting history of this area and the street art, but the guide will point out creative spaces, galleries, and foodie hotspots.

50. TAKE THE PERFECT INSTAGRAM PHOTO AT BLOUBERG BEACH

On many tourism brochures and advertisements, you see a photo of Table Bay, the city and the whole of Table Mountain including Lions Head and Devils Peak, but during your stay in Cape Town, you just cannot seem to find the angle to get that perfect shot. The secret is to travel 20 minutes north to the suburb of Blouberg, meaning Blue Mountain, and when you get there that full view will come into your eyes. Blouberg has a great beach and stunning views over the bay towards Table Mountain, and Robben Island looks like it is only a stone's throw away. Kite surfers love Blouberg and you will enjoy watching them in the waves, they even add a splash of colour on your ideal holiday photo. Pro tip: Go late afternoon, the sunset is spectacular from this angle.

51. BONUS TIP – RELAX!

Traveling can be hard work, especially if there is so much to do and see in a place like Cape Town. After all these adventures on my to-do list, enjoy an off day or afternoon and treat yourself to a day at the spa. Cape Town is well known for its retreats and spas, and there are hundreds of excellent options around. The ultimate spa experience must be at the Twelve Apostles Hotel. The views are out of this world and the spa menu offers a wide range of wellness treatments that will leave you purified, pampered and relaxed.

>TOURIST

TOP REASONS TO BOOK THIS TRIP

Adventure: With the mountain in the middle of the city and the ocean surrounding the city, Cape Town is an adventure traveller's dream destination.

Food: The food in Cape Town is stunning and definitely a highlight. You experience so much of a country and a culture through food. There are incredible options for every taste and budget, from fine dining to street food.

Culture & People: With such a rich history and with people and cultures coming together from all parts of the world, a highlight of any trip to Cape Town is experiencing the lively and diverse culture.

Nature & Wildlife: Cape Town is surrounded by Nature Reserves and National Parks. The natural environment, climate, and wildlife are incredible here. The indigenous "fynbos" vegetation that covers the mountains around Cape Town forms part of the Cape Floral Kingdom, which is the world's smallest floral kingdom in size, but has the world's biggest concentration of plants in one area. There are over 9000 different plant species, 70% of which are endemic to the area.

Enjoy your time in our beautiful city.

Greetings from Cape Town

Hendrik Human

>TOURIST

PACKING AND PLANNING TIPS

A Week before Leaving

- Arrange for someone to take care of pets and water plants.
- Email and Print important Documents.
- Get Visa and vaccines if needed.
- Check for travel warnings.
- Stop mail and newspaper.
- Notify Credit Card companies where you are going.
- Passports and photo identification is up to date.
- Pay bills.
- Copy important items and download travel Apps.
- Start collecting small bills for tips.
- Have post office hold mail while you are away.
- Check weather for the week.
- Car inspected, oil is changed, and tires have the correct pressure.
- Check airline luggage restrictions.
- Download Apps needed for your trip.

Right Before Leaving

- Contact bank and credit cards to tell them your location.
- Clean out refrigerator.
- Empty garbage cans.
- Lock windows.
- Make sure you have the proper identification with you.
- Bring cash for tips.
- Remember travel documents.
- Lock door behind you.
- Remember wallet.
- Unplug items in house and pack chargers.
- Change your thermostat settings.
- Charge electronics, and prepare camera memory cards.

>TOURIST

READ OTHER GREATER THAN A TOURIST BOOKS

Greater Than a Tourist- California: 50 Travel Tips from Locals

Greater Than a Tourist- Salem Massachusetts USA 50 Travel Tips from a Local by Danielle Lasher

Greater Than a Tourist United States: 50 Travel Tips from Locals

Greater Than a Tourist- St. Croix US Birgin Islands USA: 50 Travel Tips from a Local by Tracy Birdsall

Greater Than a Tourist- Montana: 50 Travel Tips from a Local by Laurie White

Children's Book: Charlie the Cavalier Travels the World by Lisa Rusczyk Ed. D.

> TOURIST

Follow us on Instagram for beautiful travel images:
http://Instagram.com/GreaterThanATourist

Follow *Greater Than a Tourist* on Amazon.

CZYKPublishing.com

> TOURIST

At *Greater Than a Tourist*, we love to share travel tips with you. How did we do? What guidance do you have for how we can give you better advice for your next trip? Please send your feedback to GreaterThanaTourist@gmail.com as we continue to improve the series. We appreciate your constructive feedback. Thank you.

>TOURIST

METRIC CONVERSIONS

TEMPERATURE

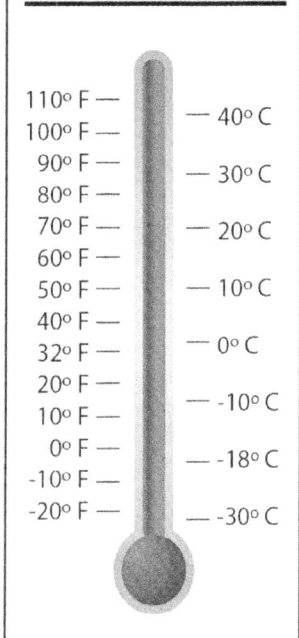

110° F — — 40° C
100° F —
90° F — — 30° C
80° F —
70° F — — 20° C
60° F —
50° F — — 10° C
40° F —
32° F — — 0° C
20° F —
10° F — — -10° C
0° F —
 — -18° C
-10° F —
-20° F — — -30° C

To convert F to C:

Subtract 32, and then multiply by 5/9 or .5555.

To Convert C to F:
Multiply by 1.8 and then add 32.

32F = 0C

LIQUID VOLUME

To Convert:................Multiply by
U.S. Gallons to Liters................ 3.8
U.S. Liters to Gallons 26
Imperial Gallons to U.S. Gallons 1.2
Imperial Gallons to Liters....... 4.55
Liters to Imperial Gallons 22

1 Liter = .26 U.S. Gallon
1 U.S. Gallon = 3.8 Liters

DISTANCE

To convert ....Multiply by
Inches to Centimeters 2.54
Centimeters to Inches 39
Feet to Meters........................3
Meters to Feet 3.28
Yards to Meters 91
Meters to Yards 1.09
Miles to Kilometers 1.61
Kilometers to Miles............ .62

1 Mile = 1.6 km
1 km = .62 Miles

WEIGHT

1 Ounce = .28 Grams
1 Pound = .4555 Kilograms
1 Gram = .04 Ounce
1 Kilogram = 2.2 Pounds

>TOURIST

TRAVEL QUESTIONS

- Do you bring presents home to family or friends after a vacation?
- Do you get motion sick?
- Do you have a favorite billboard?
- Do you know what to do if there is a flat tire?
- Do you like a sun roof open?
- Do you like to eat in the car?
- Do you like to wear sun glasses in the car?
- Do you like toppings on your ice cream?
- Do you use public bathrooms?
- Did you bring a cell phone and does it have power?
- Do you have a form of identification with you?
- Have you ever been pulled over by a cop?
- Have you ever given money to a stranger on a road trip?
- Have you ever taken a road trip with animals?
- Have you ever gone on a vacation alone?
- Have you ever run out of gas?

- If you could move to any place in the world, where would it be?
- If you could travel anywhere in the world, where would you travel?
- If you could travel in any vehicle, which one would it be?
- If you had three things to wish for from a magic genie, what would they be?
- If you have a driver's license, how many times did it take you to pass the test?
- What are you the most afraid of on vacation?
- What do you want to get away from the most when you are on vacation?
- What foods smell bad to you?
- What item do you bring on ever trip with you away from home?
- What makes you sleepy?
- What song would you love to hear on the radio when you're cruising on the highway?
- What travel job would you want the least?
- What will you miss most while you are away from home?
- What is something you always wanted to try?

>TOURIST

- What is the best road side attraction that you ever saw?
- What is the farthest distance you ever biked?
- What is the farthest distance you ever walked?
- What is the weirdest thing you needed to buy while on vacation?
- What is your favorite candy?
- What is your favorite color car?
- What is your favorite family vacation?
- What is your favorite food?
- What is your favorite gas station drink or food?
- What is your favorite license plate design?
- What is your favorite restaurant?
- What is your favorite smell?
- What is your favorite song?
- What is your favorite sound that nature makes?
- What is your favorite thing to bring home from a vacation?
- What is your favorite vacation with friends?
- What is your favorite way to relax?
- Where is the farthest place you ever traveled in a car?

- Where is the farthest place you ever went North, South, East and West?
- Where is your favorite place in the world?
- Who is your favorite singer?
- Who taught you how to drive?
- Who will you miss the most while you are away?
- Who if the first person you will contact when you get to your destination?
- Who brought you on your first vacation?
- Who likes to travel the most in your life?
- Would you rather be hot or cold?
- Would you rather drive above, below, or at the speed limited?
- Would you rather drive on a highway or a back road?
- Would you rather go on a train or a boat?
- Would you rather go to the beach or the woods?

>TOURIST

TRAVEL BUCKET LIST

1.

2.

3.

4.

5.

6.

7.

8.

9.

10.

>TOURIST

NOTES

Printed in Great Britain
by Amazon